XAIPE

By E. E. Cummings
In Liveright paperback

The Enormous Room

Etcetera: The Unpublished Poems

is 5

Selected Poems

Tulips & Chimneys

ViVa

XAIPE

In Liveright Clothbound

Complete Poems 1904–1962

XAIPE

E. E. Cummings

Edited, with an Afterword, by George James Firmage

LIVERIGHT

New York • London

Reissued in Liveright paperback 1997
Copyright 1950 by E. E. Cummings
Copyright © 1979, 1978, 1973 by Nancy T. Andrews
Copyright © 1979, 1973 by George James Firmage

Library of Congress Cataloging in Publication Data

Cummings, Edward Estlin, 1894-1962.
  (Chaire.)
  χαιρε
  (The Cummings typescript editions)
  In English.
  I. Firmage, George James. II. Title. III. Series.
PS3505.U334C5   1979   811'. 5   79–1506

ISBN 0-87140-168-1

Liveright Publishing Corporation
500 Fifth Avenue, N.Y., N.Y. 10110
W. W. Norton & Company Ltd.
10 Coptic Street, London WC1A 1PU

1 2 3 4 5 6 7 8 9 0

CONTENTS

XAIPE

to
hildegarde
watson

I

this(let's remember)day died again and
again;whose golden,crimson dooms conceive

an oceaning abyss of orange dream

larger than sky times earth:a flame beyond
soul immemorially forevering am—
and as collapsing that grey mind by wave
doom disappeared,out of perhaps(who knows?)

eternity floated a blossoming

(while anyone might slowly count to soon)
rose—did you see her?darling,did you(kiss
me)quickly count to never?you were wrong

—then all the way from perfect nowhere came

(as easily as we forget something)
livingest the imaginable moon

2

hush)
noones
are coming
out in the gloam
ing together are
standing together un
der a particular tree
are all breathing bright darkness to
gether are slowly all together

very magically smiling and if

we are not perfectly careful be
lieve me you and i'll go strolling
right through these each illimit
able to speak very
softly altogeth
er miracu
lous citi
zens of
(hush

3

purer than purest pure
whisper of a whisper

so(big with innocence)
forgivingly a once
of eager glory,no
more miracle may grow

—childfully serious
flower of holiness

a pilgrim from beyond
the future's future;and
immediate like some
newly remembered dream—

flaming a coolly bell
touches most mere until

(eternally)with(now)
luminous the shadow
of love himself:who's we
—nor can you die or i

and every world,before
silence begins a star

4

this out of within itself moo
ving lump of twilight squirts a two
ne like nothing verdi slightly knu

as and some six cents hit the whigh
shaped hathole thangew yelps one shi
ly glad old unman who is eye

5

swim so now million many worlds in each

least less than particle of perfect dark—
how should a loudness called mankind unteach
whole infinite the who of life's life(hark

what silence)?"   "Worlds? o no:i'm certain they're
(look again)flowers."   "Don't worlds open and
worlds close?"   "Worlds do,but differently;or

as if worlds wanted us to understand
they'd never close(and open)if that fool
called everyone(or you or i)were wise."

"You mean worlds may have better luck,some day?"
"Or worse!poor worlds;i mean they're possible
—but" lifting "flowers" more all stars than eyes

"only are quite what worlds merely might be

6

dying is fine)but Death

?o
baby
i

wouldn't like

Death if Death
were
good:for

when(instead of stopping to think)you

begin to feel of it,dying
's miraculous
why?be

cause dying is

perfectly natural;perfectly
putting
it mildly lively(but

Death

is strictly
scientific
& artificial &

evil & legal)

we thank thee
god
almighty for dying

(forgive us,o life!the sin of Death

7

we miss you,jack—tactfully you(with one cocked
eyebrow)subtracting clichés un by un
till the god's truth stands art-naked:you and the fact

that rotgut never was brewed which could knock you down

(while scotch was your breakfast every night all day)
a 3ringbrain you had and a circusheart
and we miss them more than any bright word may cry
—even the crackling spark of(hung in a)"fert

ig"
    (tent-sky wholly wallendas)
                                    ready were all

erect your yous to cross the chasm of time
lessness;but two dim disks of stare are still
wondering if the stunt was really a dream—

here's,wherever you aren't or are,good luck!
aberdeen plato-rabelais peter jack

8

o

the round
little man we
loved so isn't

no!w

a gay of a
brave and
a true of a

who have

r
olle
d i

nt

o
n
o

w(he)re

9

possibly thrice we glimpsed—
                              more likely twice
that(once crammed into someone's kitchenette)

wheezing bulgily world of genial plac
-idity(plus,out of much its misbutt-
oned trouserfly tumbling,faded five
or so lightyears of pyjamastring)

a(vastly and particularly)live
that undeluded notselfpitying

lover of all things excellently rare;
obsolete almost that phenomenon
(too gay for malice and too wise for fear)
of shadowy virtue and of sunful sin

namely(ford madox ford)and eke to wit
a human being
                    —let's remember that

10

or who and who)

The distance is
more much than all
of timely space
(was and be will)
from beautiful

obvious to

Mere but one small
most of a rose
easily(while
will be goes was)
can travel this

or i and you

so many selves(so many fiends and gods
each greedier than every)is a man
(so easily one in another hides;
yet man can,being all,escape from none)

so huge a tumult is the simplest wish:
so pitiless a massacre the hope
most innocent(so deep's the mind of flesh
and so awake what waking calls asleep)

so never is most lonely man alone
(his briefest breathing lives some planet's year,
his longest life's a heartbeat of some sun;
his least unmotion roams the youngest star)

—how should a fool that calls him "I" presume
to comprehend not numerable whom?

12

tw

o o
ld
o

nce upo

n
a(
n

o mo

re
)time
me

n

sit(l
oo
k)dre

am

13

chas sing does(who
,ins
tead,
smiles alw

ays a trifl
e
w
hile ironin

g!
nob odyknowswhos esh
?i
rt)n't

14

out of more find than seeks

thinking,swim(opening)grow
are(me wander and nows to the

power of blueness)whos(ex-
plore my unreal in

-credible true each new

self)smile. Eyes. & we
remember:yes;we played with a piece of when

till it rolled behind forever, we touched a shy
animal called where and she disappeared.

Out of more(fingeryhands

me and whying)seek than finds
feeling(seize)floats(only by

only)a silence only made of,bird

hair your a brook
(it through are gaze
the unguessed whys
by me at look)

swirls to engulf
(in which in soft)
firm who outlift
queries of self

pouring(alive
twice)and becomes
eithering dreams
the secret of

16

if the

green
opens
a little a
little
was
much and much
is

too if

the green robe
o
p
e
n
s
and two are

wildstrawberries

17

(swooning)a pillar of youngly

loveflesh topped
with danc
ing egghead strutstrolls

eager a(twice

by
Dizzying eyeplums
pun

ctured)moo

nface swimming
ly
dreamseems

(vivi

d
an O
of

milky tranceworld writhes

in
twi
nn

ingly scarlet woundsmile)

a(ncient)a

weigh
tless

puppet of once
man(clutched
by immense

the-seat-of-the
pants
inani
nvisible Fist)drifts

a
long conway
's

unstreet with
treadwatering

nonlegs(strictly)smiling

19

out of the mountain of his soul comes
a keen pure silence)such hands can
build a(who are like ocean patient)dream's

eternity(you feel behind this man
earth's first sunrise)and his voice
is green like growing(is miraculous like
tomorrow)all around the self of this

being are growing stones(neither awake
are goddesses nor sleeping)since he's young
with mysteries(each truly his more than
some eighty years through which that memory strolls)
and every ours for the mere worshipping

(as calmly as if aristide maillols
occurred with any ticking of a clock

20

goo–dmore–ning(en

ter)nize–aday(most
gently herculanean

my mortal)yoo

make sno eye kil
yoo(friend the laughing
grinning)we

no(smiling)strike

agains
De Big Boss
(crying)jew wop
rich poor(sing

ing)

He
    no
        care
            so
                what

yoo–gointa–doo?(ice

coal wood
man)nic
he like
wint–air

nic like ot–am

sum-air(young
old nic)
like spring yoo

un-air-stan?me

crazy
me like

evry-ting

21

jake hates
　　　all the girls(the
shy ones,the bold
ones;the meek
proud sloppy sleek)
all except the cold
　　　　　ones

paul scorns all
　　　　　the girls(the
bright ones,the dim
ones;the slim
plump tiny tall)
all except the
　　　dull ones

gus loves all the
　　　　　girls(the
warped ones,the lamed
ones;the mad
moronic maimed)
all except
　　　the dead ones

mike likes all the girls
　　　　　(the
fat ones,the lean
ones;the mean
kind dirty clean)
all
　　except the green ones

22

when serpents bargain for the right to squirm
and the sun strikes to gain a living wage—
when thorns regard their roses with alarm
and rainbows are insured against old age

when every thrush may sing no new moon in
if all screech-owls have not okayed his voice
—and any wave signs on the dotted line
or else an ocean is compelled to close

when the oak begs permission of the birch
to make an acorn—valleys accuse their
mountains of having altitude—and march
denounces april as a saboteur

then we'll believe in that incredible
unanimal mankind(and not until)

23

three wealthy sisters swore they'd never part:
Soul was(i understand)
seduced by Life;whose brother married Heart,
now Mrs Death.   Poor Mind

24

one day a nigger
caught in his hand
a little star no bigger
than not to understand

"i'll never let you go
until you've made me white"
so she did and now
stars shine at night

25

pieces(in darker
than small is dirtiest
any city's least
street)of mirror

lying are each(why
do people say it's un
lucky to break one)
whole with sky

26

who sharpens every dull
here comes the only man
reminding with his bell
to disappear a sun

and out of houses pour
maids mothers widows wives
bringing this visitor
their very oldest lives

one pays him with a smile
another with a tear
some cannot pay at all
he never seems to care

he sharpens is to am
he sharpens say to sing
you'd almost cut your thumb
so right he sharpens wrong

and when their lives are keen
he throws the world a kiss
and slings his wheel upon
his back and off he goes

but we can hear him still
if now our sun is gone
reminding with his bell
to reappear a moon

27

"summer is over
—it's no use demanding
that lending be giving;
it's no good pretending
befriending means loving"
(sighs mind:and he's clever)
"for all,yes for all
sweet things are until"

"spring follows winter:
as clover knows,maybe"
(heart makes the suggestion)
"or even a daisy—
your thorniest question
my roses will answer"
"but dying's meanwhile"
(mind murmurs;the fool)

"truth would prove truthless
and life a mere pastime
—each joy a deceiver,
and sorrow a system—
if now than forever
could never(by breathless
one breathing)be" soul
"more" cries:with a smile

28

noone" autumnal this great lady's gaze

enters a sunset "can grow(gracefully or
otherwise)old.   Old may mean anything
which everyone would rather not become;
but growing is" erect her whole life smiled

"was and will always remain:who i am.

Look at these(each serenely welcoming
his only and illimitably his
destiny)mountains!how can each" while flame
crashed "be so am and i and who?each grows"

then in a whisper,as time turned to dream

"and poets grow;and(there—see?)children" nor
might any earth's first morning have concealed
so unimaginably young a star

29

nine birds(rising

through a gold moment)climb:
ing i

-nto
wintry
twi-

light
(all together a
manying
one

-ness)nine
souls
only alive with a single mys-

tery(liftingly
caught upon falling)silent!

ly living the dying of glory

30

snow means that

life is a black cannonadin
g into silenc
e go

lliw

og-dog)life
?
tree3ghosts

are Is A eyes

Strange
known
Face

(whylaughing!among:skydiamonds

infinite jukethrob smoke & swallow to dis

gorge)
      a sulky gob with entirely white
eyes of elsewhere
           jabber while(infinite
fog & puking jukepulse hug)large less
than more magnetic pink unwhores
               a wai
ter lugs his copious whichwhat skilfully here
&(simply infinite)there &
           (smoke)a fair
y socked flopslump(& juke)ing shrieks Yew May
n't Dew Thiz Tew Mee
           as somebody's almost moth
er folds(but infinite)gently up
           the with
a carroty youth blonde whis(gorgedis reswal
lowing spewnonspew clutch)pers again & again
(jukejog mist & strict)
         & again
           (ly infin)

It's Snowing Isn't That Perfectly Wonderful

32

blossoming are people

nimbler than Really
go whirling into gaily

white thousands return

by millions and dreaming

drift hundreds come swimming
(Each a keener secret

than silence even tells)

all the earth has turned to sky

are flowers neither why nor how
when is now and which is Who

and i am you are i am we

(pretty twinkle merry bells)

Someone has been born
everyone is noone

dance around the snowman

33

if a cheerfulest Elephantangelchild should sit

(holding a red candle over his head
by a finger of trunk,and singing out of a red

book)on a proud round cloud in a white high night

where his heartlike ears have flown adorable him
self tail and all(and his tail's red christmas bow)
—and if,when we meet again,little he(having flown
even higher)is sunning his penguinsoul in the glow

of a joy which wasn't and isn't and won't be words

while possibly not(at a guess)quite half way down
to the earth are leapandswooping tinily birds
whose magical gaiety makes your beautiful name—

i feel that(false and true are merely to know)
Love only has ever been,is,and will ever be,So

34

a thrown a

-way It
with some-
thing sil
-very

;bright,&:mys(

a thrown a-
way
X
-mas)ter-

i

-ous wisp A of glo-
ry.pr
-ettily
cl(tr)in(ee)gi-

ng

35

light's lives lurch
                    a once world quickly from rises

army the gradual of unbeing(fro
on stiffening greenly air and to ghosts go
drift slippery hands tease slim float twitter faces)
only stand with me,love!against these its
until you are and until i am dreams

until comes vast dark until sink last things

(least all turns almost now;now almost swims
into a hair's width:into less?into

not)
      love,stand with me while silence sings

not into nothing and nothing into never
and never into(touch me!love)forever
—until is and shall be and was are night's

total exploding millionminded Who

36

quick i the death of thing
glimpsed(and on every side
swoop mountains flimsying
become if who'd)

me under a opens
(of petals of silence)
hole bigger than
never to have been

what above did was
always fall
(yes but behind yes)
without or until

no atom couldn't die
(how and am quick i
they'll all not conceive
less who than love)

F is for foetus(a

punkslapping
mobsucking
gravypissing poppa but
who just couldn't help it no

matter how hard he never tried)the

great pink
superme
diocri
ty of

a hyperhypocritical D

mocra
c(sing
down with the fascist beast
boom

boom)two eyes

for an eye four
teeth for a tooth
(and the wholly babble open at
blessed are the peacemuckers)

$ $ $ etc(as

the boodle's bent is the
crowd inclined it's
freedom from freedom
the common man wants)

honey swoRkey mollypants

38

why must itself up every of a park

anus stick some quote statue unquote to
prove that a hero equals any jerk
who was afraid to dare to answer "no"?

quote citizens unquote might otherwise
forget(to err is human;to forgive
divine)that if the quote state unquote says
"kill" killing is an act of christian love.

"Nothing" in 1944 A D

"can stand against the argument of mil
itary necessity"(generalissimo e)
and echo answers "there is no appeal

from reason"(freud)—you pays your money and
you doesn't take your choice.   Ain't freedom grand

39

open his head,baby
& you'll find a heart in it
(cracked)

open that heart,mabel
& you'll find a bed in it
(fact)

open this bed,sibyl
& you'll find a tart in it
(wed)

open the tart,lady
& you'll find his mind in it
(dead)

i'm
asking
you dear to
what else could a
no but it doesn't
of course but you don't seem
to realize i can't make
it clearer war just isn't what
we imagine but please for god's O
what the hell yes it's true that was
me but that me isn't me
can't you see now no not
any christ but you
must understand
why because
i am
dead

whose are these(wraith a clinging with a wraith)

ghosts drowning in supreme thunder?ours
(over you reels and me a moon;beneath,

bombed the by ocean earth bigly shudders)

never was death so alive:chaos so(hark
—that screech of space)absolute(my soul
tastes If as some world of a spark

's gulped by illimitable hell)

and never have breathed such miracle murdered we
whom cannot kill more mostful to arrive
each(futuring snowily which sprints for the
crumb of our Now)twiceuponatime wave—

put out your eyes,and touch the black skin
of an angel named imagination

42

neither awake
(there's your general
yas buy gad)
nor asleep

booted & spurred
with an apish grin
(extremely like
but quite absurd

gloved fist on hip
& the scowl of a cannibal)
there's your mineral
general animal

(five foot five)
neither dead
nor alive
(in real the rain)

43

o to be in finland
now that russia's here)

swing low
sweet ca

rr
y on

(pass the freedoms pappy or
uncle shylock not interested

44

where's Jack Was
General Was
the hero of the Battle of Because
    he's squatting
in the middle of remember
with his rotten old forgotten
full of why
    (rub–her–bub)
    bub?
    (bubs)

where's Jim Soon
Admiral Soon
the saviour of the Navy of the Moon
    he's swooning
at the bottom of the ocean
of forever with a never
in his fly
    (rub–her–bub)
    bub?
    (bubs)

where's John Big
Doughgob Big
pastmaster of the Art of Jigajig
    sitting pretty
on the top of notwithstanding
with his censored up a wench's
rock-a-bye
    (rub–her–bub)
    bub ?
    (bubs)

45

when your honest redskin toma
hawked and scalped his victim ,

not to save a world for stalin
was he aiming ;

spare the child and spoil the rod
quoth the palmist .

a kike is the most dangerous
machine as yet invented
by even yankee ingenu
ity(out of a jew a few
dead dollars and some twisted laws)
it comes both prigged and canted

47

meet mr universe(who clean

and jerked 300 lbs)i mean
observe his these regard his that(sh)

who made the world's best one hand snatch

48

&(all during the

dropsin
king god my sic
kly a thingish o crashdis
appearing con ter fusion ror collap
sing thatthis is whichwhat yell itfulls o
f cringewiltdroolery i
mean really th
underscream of sudde
nly perishing eagerly everyw
here shutting forever&forever fol
ding int
o absolute gone &
positive quite n
ever & bi
g screeching new black perfectly isn

't)one rose opened

49

this is a rubbish of human rind
with a photograph
clutched in the half
of a hand and the word
love underlined

this is a girl who died in her mind
with a warm thick scream
and a keen cold groan
while the gadgets purred
and the gangsters dined

this is a deaf dumb church and blind
with an if in its soul
and a hole in its life
where the young bell tolled
and the old vine twined

this is a dog of no known kind
with one white eye
and one black eye
and the eyes of his eyes
are as lost as you'll find

50

no time ago
or else a life
walking in the dark
i met christ

jesus)my heart
flopped over
and lay still
while he passed(as

close as i'm to you
yes closer
made of nothing
except loneliness

who were so dark of heart they might not speak,
a little innocence will make them sing;
teach them to see who could not learn to look
—from the reality of all nothing

will actually lift a luminous whole;
turn sheer despairing to most perfect gay,
nowhere to here,never to beautiful:
a little innocence creates a day.

And something thought or done or wished without
a little innocence,although it were
as red as terror and as green as fate,
greyly shall fail and dully disappear—

but the proud power of himself death immense
is not so as a little innocence

52

to start,to hesitate;to stop
(kneeling in doubt:while all
skies fall)and then to slowly trust
T upon H,and smile

could anything be pleasanter
(some big dark little day
which seems a lifetime at the least)
except to add an A?

henceforth he feels his pride involved
(this i who's also you)
and nothing less than excellent
E will exactly do

next(our great problem nearly solved)
we dare adorn the whole
with a distinct grandiloquent
deep D;while all skies fall

at last perfection,now and here
—but look:not sunlight?yes!
and(plunging rapturously up)
we spill our masterpiece

53

mighty guest of merely me

—traveller from eternity;
in a single wish,receive
all i am and dream and have.

Be thou gay by dark and day:
gay as only truth is gay
(nothing's false,in earth in air
in water and in fire,but fear—

mind's a coward;lies are laws)
laugh,and make each no thy yes:
love;and give because the why

—gracious wanderer,be thou gay

54

maybe god

is a child
's hand)very carefully
bring
-ing
to you and to
me(and quite with
out crushing)the

papery weightless diminutive

world
with a hole in
it out
of which demons with wings would be streaming if
something had(maybe they couldn't
agree)not happened(and floating-
ly int

o

55

(fea
therr
ain

:dreamin
g field o
ver forest &;

wh
o could
be

so
!f!
te

r?n
oo
ne)

56

a like a
grey
rock wanderin

g
through
pasture
wom

an creature whom
than
earth hers

elf
could
silent more no
be

57

(im)c-a-t(mo)
b,i;l:e

FallleA
ps!fl
OattumblI

sh?dr
IftwhirlF
(Ul)(lY)
&&&

away wanders:exact
ly;as if
not
hing had,ever happ
ene

D

after screamgroa
ning.ish:ly;
come

    (s

gruntsqueak
,while,
idling-is-grindstone

one;what:of.thumb

stutt(er(s a)mu)ddied
bushscytheblade
"pud-dih-gud"

)S

creang
roami
ngis

59

the little horse is newlY

Born)he knows nothing,and feels
everything;all around whom is

perfectly a strange
ness(Of sun
light and of fragrance and of

Singing)is ev
erywhere(a welcom
ing dream:is amazing)
a worlD.and in

this world lies:smoothbeautifuL
ly folded;a(brea
thing and a gro

Wing)silence,who;
is:somE

oNe.

60

(nothing whichful about

thick big this
friendly
himself of
a boulder)nothing

mean in tenderly

whoms
of sizeless a
silence by noises
called people called

sunlight

(elsewhere flat the mechanical
itmaking
sickness of mind sprawls)
here

a livingly free mysterious

dreamsoul floatstands
oak by birch by maple
pine
by hemlock spruce by

tamarack(

nothing pampered puny
impatient
and nothing
ignoble

)everywhere wonder

61

if(touched by love's own secret)we,like homing
through welcoming sweet miracles of air
(and joyfully all truths of wing resuming)
selves,into infinite tomorrow steer

—souls under whom flow(mountain valley forest)
a million wheres which never may become
one(wholly strange;familiar wholly)dearest
more than reality of more than dream—

how should contented fools of fact envision
the mystery of freedom?yet,among
their loud exactitudes of imprecision,
you'll(silently alighting)and i'll sing

while at us very deafly a most stares
colossal hoax of clocks and calendars

62

in

Spring comes(no-
one
asks his name)

a mender
of things

with eager
fingers(with
patient
eyes)re

-new-

ing remaking what
other
-wise we should
have
thrown a-

way(and whose

brook
-bright flower-
soft bird
-quick voice loves

children
and sunlight and

mountains)in april(but
if he should
Smile)comes

nobody'll know

63

honour corruption villainy holiness
riding in fragrance of sunlight(side by side
all in a singing wonder of blossoming yes
riding)to him who died that death should be dead

humblest and proudest eagerly wandering
(equally all alive in miraculous day)
merrily moving through sweet forgiveness of spring
(over the under the gift of the earth of the sky

knight and ploughman pardoner wife and nun
merchant frere clerk somnour miller and reve
and geoffrey and all)come up from the never of when
come into the now of forever come riding alive

down while crylessly drifting through vast most
nothing's own nothing children go of dust

64

the of an it ignoblest he
to nowhere from arrive
human the most catastrophe
april might make alive

filthy some past imagining
whowhich of mad rags strode
earth ignorantly blossoming
a scarecrow demongod

countless in hatred pity fear
each more exactly than
the other un good people stare
for it or he is one

65

i thank You God for most this amazing
day:for the leaping greenly spirits of trees
and a blue true dream of sky;and for everything
which is natural which is infinite which is yes

(i who have died am alive again today,
and this is the sun's birthday;this is the birth
day of life and of love and wings:and of the gay
great happening illimitably earth)

how should tasting touching hearing seeing
breathing any—lifted from the no
of all nothing—human merely being
doubt unimaginable You?

(now the ears of my ears awake and
now the eyes of my eyes are opened)

66

the great advantage of being alive
(instead of undying)is not so much
that mind no more can disprove than prove
what heart may feel and soul may touch
—the great(my darling)happens to be
that love are in we,that love are in we

and here is a secret they never will share
for whom create is less than have
or one times one than when times where—
that we are in love,that we are in love:
with us they've nothing times nothing to do
(for love are in we am in i are in you)

this world(as timorous itsters all
to call their cowardice quite agree)
shall never discover our touch and feel
—for love are in we are in love are in we;
for you are and i am and we are(above
and under all possible worlds)in love

a billion brains may coax undeath
from fancied fact and spaceful time—
no heart can leap,no soul can breathe
but by the sizeless truth of a dream
whose sleep is the sky and the earth and the sea.
For love are in you am in i are in we

when faces called flowers float out of the ground
and breathing is wishing and wishing is having—
but keeping is downward and doubting and never
—it's april(yes,april;my darling)it's spring!
yes the pretty birds frolic as spry as can fly
yes the little fish gambol as glad as can be
(yes the mountains are dancing together)

when every leaf opens without any sound
and wishing is having and having is giving—
but keeping is doting and nothing and nonsense
—alive;we're alive,dear:it's(kiss me now)spring!
now the pretty birds hover so she and so he
now the little fish quiver so you and so i
(now the mountains are dancing,the mountains)

when more than was lost has been found has been found
and having is giving and giving is living—
but keeping is darkness and winter and cringing
—it's spring(all our night becomes day)o,it's spring!
all the pretty birds dive to the heart of the sky
all the little fish climb through the mind of the sea
(all the mountains are dancing;are dancing)

68

love our so right
is,all(each thing
most lovely)sweet
things cannot spring
but we be they'll

some or if where
shall breathe a new
(silverly rare`
goldenly so)
moon,she is you

nothing may,quite
your my(my your
and)self without,
completely dare
be beautiful

one if should sing
(at yes of day)
younger than young
bird first for joy,
he's i he's i

69

now all the fingers of this tree(darling)have
hands,and all the hands have people;and
more each particular person is(my love)
alive than every world can understand

and now you are and i am now and we're
a mystery which will never happen again,
a miracle which has never happened before—
and shining this our now must come to then

our then shall be some darkness during which
fingers are without hands;and i have no
you:and all trees are(any more than each
leafless)its silent in forevering snow

—but never fear(my own,my beautiful
my blossoming)for also then's until

70

blue the triangular why

of a dream(with
crazily
eyes of window)may

be un

less it
were(floati
ng through

never)a kite

like face of
the child who's
every

child(&

therefore invisible)anyhow you
've(whoever
we are)stepped carefully o

ver(& i)some

newer
than life(or than
death)is on

f

ilthi
es
t

sidewalk blossoming glory

luminous tendril of celestial wish

(whying diminutive bright deathlessness
to these my not themselves believing eyes
adventuring,enormous nowhere from)

querying affirmation;virginal

immediacy of precision:more
and perfectly more most ethereal
silence through twilight's mystery made flesh—

dreamslender exquisite white firstful flame

—new moon!as(by the miracle of your
sweet innocence refuted)clumsy some
dull cowardice called a world vanishes,

teach disappearing also me the keen
illimitable secret of begin

AFTERWORD

by

George James Firmage

The title of E. E. Cummings' tenth "bookofpoems" is the Greek salutation "χαιρε." It means "greetings" or "rejoice" and, in its simplest English transliteration, can be written as "khi-ra" with the accent on the first syllable.

According to his letter of August 23,1949, to Ezra Pound, Cummings "spent several months persuading (espérons) 71 poems to make 1 book who called himself xaîpe. Now et comment," he continued, "The quote Oxford unquote Press registers alarm nudging horror; poems are nonsellable enough (paraît) without calling the poembook by some foreign word which no Good-American could either spell or pronounce."[1] This would explain the presence of the subtitle "seventy-one poems" in the edition as published by Oxford on March 30, 1950. As Cummings later recalled, "the publisher . . . was responsible for this addendum."[2]

XAIPE is dedicated to Hildegarde Watson, the wife of Cummings' lifelong friend James Sibley Watson, Jr. It was Watson who, together with Scofield Thayer, took over *The Dial* in 1919 and changed it into a vigorous monthly magazine devoted to "art and literature." The first issue of the

1. *Selected Letters of E. E. Cummings* (New York: Harcourt Brace & World, Inc., 1969), p. 193.
2. Charles Norman, *The Magic-Maker: E. E. Cummings* (New York: The Macmillan Company, 1958), p. 381.

newly constituted periodical appeared in January 1920 and marked the professional debut of E. E. Cummings as a poet and an artist.

With a single exception, the present edition of *XAIPE* is based on the poet's final and complete typescript,[3] and two sets of corrected proofs and a list of "ERRORS"[4] prepared for the book's first publisher which are all in the Houghton Library, Harvard University. The exception, poem 59, is stylistically inconsistent in its use of the parenthesis. The version published here has been corrected against an earlier manuscript in the Houghton's collection.[5]

3. bMs Am 1823.4 (98).
4. bMs Am 1823.4 (101) and bMs Am 1823.4 (102).
5. bMs Am 1823.5 (353).